ODD CORNERS *of the* LONDON MIDLAND *from the Days of Steam*

Ivatt 2MT 2–6–0 no. 46404 pictured leaving Huntingdon East for Cambridge.

16.3.54

ODD CORNERS *of the*
LONDON MIDLAND
from the Days of Steam

ERIC SAWFORD

SUTTON PUBLISHING

First published in 2003 by
Sutton Publishing Limited · Phoenix Mill
Thrupp · Stroud · Gloucestershire · GL5 2BU

British Library Cataloguing in Publication Data
A catalogue record for this book is available from the British Library

ISBN 0-7509-3220-1

Half-title page photograph: Two WD 2–8–0s fresh from general overhaul at Crewe works wait to be reunited with their tenders. In the background, also fresh from works, is 'Jubilee' class no. 45633 *Aden* from Preston depot.

12.8.52

Title page photograph: LMS Standard 3F 0–6–0T no. 47313 was one of seven shunting engines built for the Somerset & Dorset Joint Railway in 1929 and was later taken into LMS stock. This engine was used as one of the Lickey bankers and is seen here at Bromsgrove shed.

17.7.53

Endpapers. Front: Class 2P 4–4–0 no. 40493 leaving Nottingham depot passes an old locomotive tender given a new lease of life as a sludge-carrier. Such tenders were modified to carry the lime deposits from water-softening plants for disposal.

4.4.54

Back: Class 9F 2–10–0s were still to be seen at Wellingborough until the shed finally closed. This is no. 92073. Note the flangeless middle set of driving wheels.

17.10.65

Typeset in 10/12pt Palatino.
Typesetting and origination by
Sutton Publishing Limited.
Printed and bound in England by
J.H. Haynes & Co. Ltd, Sparkford.

Contents

Webb 2–4–2T no. 46680 was nearing the end of its long working life, engaged on shunting work at Crewe North shed. The engine was withdrawn in February 1953. As with other members of the class it was fitted for push-pull working.

12.8.1952

Introduction

It is all too easy with hindsight to say I wish I had taken more photographs in steam days, not just of locomotives but also of the railway infrastructure that existed at the time. But quite apart from the cost of film, who thought in the 1950s that such familiar sights as steam engines, the seemingly endless heavy goods trains and the fascinating array of signals, plus numerous other subjects, would disappear in just a few years. Fortunately, I did record on film a wide selection of railway subjects, not just locomotives and trains. In this book I have put together a collection of pictures of the London Midland Region from this period, when it was certainly very different from today's railway scene.

My main interest during the 1950s and 1960s was steam locomotives, and I recorded on film any in favourable positions, irrespective of class and taking no account of such frequently heard comments as 'Oh no, not another Black 5'. Throughout my travels I was always on the look-out for engines under repair. Locomotive sheds ranged from those with well-equipped repair areas devoted entirely to this work, to those where space was very much at a premium. In the latter it was quite usual for an engine to be removed to the yard while work was carried out. As a result engines could often be seen propped up on wooden blocks, perhaps with their driving wheels, front pony truck or trailing wheels removed. Included in this book are a number of such views.

Photography inside sheds was not easy unless one had the time to use a tripod. Even then safety was a major consideration, as it was all too easy for photographers intent on getting a good picture to get in the way of the endless stream of engines moving around, or to step backwards into a pit. Some sheds were quite light buildings, while others were smoky or dark and had very little room. You could almost guarantee that if you travelled to a shed specially to photograph a particular locomotive you would find it in the very darkest part of the shed!

Travelling to distant sheds could present problems as only a few were located near stations. Fortunately, there was a very useful publication available in the form of a shed directory, which gave information on local transport, road names and so on. Some sheds were in very isolated locations and often were quite a distance from the nearest public transport point, so there was frequently a lot of walking to do. Large cities presented their own problems as they were usually served by several pre-Grouping companies, each having its own depot. There was, of course, a temptation to try to visit too many in a day, with the result that you always had to rush and usually ran out of time.

Most of the regions granted visitor permits to individual enthusiasts, the exception being the Eastern and North Eastern regions where visits were limited to organised parties. For those principally interested in photography this presented a different set of problems, as they would be competing with those who were solely interested in collecting numbers – and they could get round a shed much more quickly. Typically the organisers would hire a coach, which started out from a large station often around 5am! Looking back it must have been very difficult at times for the coach driver. The party leader could usually give directions to get to a particular shed – but the driver had to contend with narrow lanes, cramped space in which to turn and in some cases nowhere to park. On arrival, everyone would pile out of the coach ready for the off. As the number collectors raced round, the photographers simply had to snatch shots of whatever was available in a good position as time was very much against them.

The trips were often marathon events, depending on how many visits were planned, and even then it was not unknown for extra calls to be made. These were the days of curled-up sandwiches (made the previous day) and fizzy drinks. The usual procedure was to arrive back at a principal station at around 6pm. Hot, tired and dirty, everyone would then make their own way home. Those were the days!

In steam days numerous depots had a steam crane and attendant vehicles. At major depots the crane was often to be found in light steam. If a problem arose the shed

1

Nearing the end of its working life, 3P no. 41961 stands on the pits at Nottingham. This engine was a rebuild of a London, Tilbury & Southend Railway design, introduced in 1897. It was withdrawn in October 1952.

6.7.51

Three years after nationalisation ex-LNWR 'Cauliflower' no. 28585 had still not received its BR number and its tender still carried the letters LMS. This picture was taken at Rhyl where a number of these engines were to be found in the early 1950s.

2.9.51

Brand-new Standard 5MT no. 73006 stands in the shed yard at Derby undergoing steering trials before running in. In due course it would be sent to its first shed.

3.7.51

superintendent, a locomotive foreman and several fitters would man the train. These cranes varied in size, main line depots having large 45-ton units and a well-equipped back-up set. Others had much smaller and older units. Today an emergency unit comprises purpose-built vehicles. In steam days it was very different, as the crane itself, its jib truck and runners, was a special unit. Vehicles used in conjunction with the cranes were normally old coaches, often six-wheelers that had long since been taken out of public service. The majority of calls were straightforward, and derailments of locomotives or rolling stock were quickly dealt with. In a major incident two or more cranes might be called to the scene, and these would certainly be required to lift a large engine.

In the locomotive section of this book every opportunity has been taken to include pictures that show as much of the background at the depots as possible. In the case of smaller depots little was provided, and at very small sheds watering facilities and coal supplies consisted simply of a platform from where supplies were shovelled on to the locomotive. At the other end of the scale were the massive coaling plants where coal wagons were hauled up to fill a giant hopper. At these large sheds numerous water cranes were located in various parts of the yards, together with dry sand supplies. The locomotive disposal point had pits where firemen could drop ashes and clinker. These pits were very labour intensive as a member of staff later had the dirty, backbreaking job of loading the ashes into wagons.

Steam locomotives required a considerable number of maintenance staff. Men were required to light up, move engines to get them into the right position, and turn them. In addition, engines in steam required regular visits to keep sufficient steam until the booked locomotive crew took over. When an engine arrived on shed at the end of its turn of duty, further work was required, such as cleaning the fire, emptying the smokebox, coaling and

Bletchley shed roof was renewed in 1953, giving the former LNWR depot a further lease of life. This was a medium-sized shed throughout the 1950s with over fifty engines on its books. Towards the end of the decade its allocation included five Standard 4MT 4–6–0s, of which no. 75036 is seen here awaiting its next turn of duty.

15.7.54

watering. In addition, regular inspections, boiler washouts and any necessary repairs or adjustments had to be carried out, all of which served to increase the depot's labour force. Turntables were a very important part of a locomotive depot's equipment. Some were vacuum-assisted, while others still required considerable manual effort and very precise positioning of the locomotive.

In areas where the water supplies were very alkaline, water-softening plants were used to treat supplies. This process produced considerable quantities of sludge which had to be disposed of, and many old locomotive tenders were given a new lease of life for this purpose. Similar installations also existed at water troughs where the water quality was unsuitable. These old tenders were usually collected by a pick-up goods and delivered to a suitable disposal point.

One shed that I visited on numerous occasions was Bletchley. This had a small repair section that was often called upon to work on engines that had failed in the immediate vicinity. As a result locomotive types not associated with the shed were often to be seen in the repair bays. In the shed photographs section are a number of pictures indicating the wide variety of types that found their way there. Anything that could not be dealt with at Bletchley would be sent to Rugby, where a small works existed, or to Crewe works itself.

Breakdown cranes were to be found at most of the principal depots and they ranged considerably in size. This example, no. RS1025-15, built by Cowans & Sheldon, was photographed at Bletchley, its veteran six-wheel coach having been replaced with a more modern vehicle.

29.4.56

Although they were a mixed-traffic design, the Stanier 2–6–0s were not very often seen on passenger trains, especially from the mid-1950s onwards. No. 42975, pictured at Llandudno, was heading a local passenger service to Chester.

30.8.51

Rhyl shed was an excellent spot for enthusiasts in the early 1950s, with its ex-LNWR 2–4–2Ts, 0–6–2Ts (coal tanks) and 0–6–0s ('Cauliflowers'), as well as ex-Lancashire & Yorkshire Railway 0–6–0s and examples of several other classes. No. 58911 is pictured ready to leave the shed for its next duty.

3.7.51

It was not only countless steam locomotives that were condemned during the late 1950s but also large numbers of wagons and coaches. Initially engines were cut up at locomotive works, as had been the practice for a number of years. But as time went by the sheer numbers involved overwhelmed the works and as a result locomotives began to be sold to private scrapyards. This sometimes involved withdrawn engines being towed over great distances. Such were the numbers involved that during the 1960s large quantities of withdrawn engines built up, and some sheds had to allocate sidings to hold them until they could be towed away. Many had parts removed to keep others going. At this time a familiar sight was the sad procession of four or five engines on their last journey. Many of these movements were made at night, as it was far from unknown for problems to arise with engines that had stood idle for a long time.

The railway scene generally was very different in the days of steam, when vast quantities of wagons were still in use. Among the coal wagons were huge numbers that at one time were in private ownership. There were many other vehicles for particular loads, such as fruit and fish (and a loaded fish train was something you could not mistake!), even special vans for the transportation of gunpowder. In addition, there were various wagons for special loads, industrial plant, large vehicles, steel girders, bricks and many more.

Veteran coaches dating back to pre-Grouping days were still in regular use, and branch lines were always good hunting-grounds for these. Old coaches, including six-wheelers, were often to be found in the make-up of engineering trains. They were usually painted black and numbered in departmental series. Many were to see a further lease of life with breakdown sets. Others, their wheels and running gear removed, were used as stores and mess rooms.

Travelling by train during steam days was very different, especially before the Beeching era. Numerous cross-country lines were still open, as were countless wayside stations serving small communities; all of them have passed into history. Even small stations often had a signal-box. Most had a stationmaster and some could boast a few sidings and a goods shed. Wagons were received and dispatched via the daily pick-up goods. At many of these stations there was a water crane. Other once-familiar items that made up our railway infrastructure in those days included telegraph poles, linesman's huts and even unmanned crossings on branch lines where you had to open and shut the gates yourself.

The pre-Grouping railways required their signs and notices to last, and in the 1950s signs dating back to the previous century were still commonplace. Many were made of cast-iron, and withstood years of exposure to the elements with nothing more to protect them than the occasional coat of paint. These castings were, however, brittle and could be broken or cracked by a heavy blow. The numbers produced must have been colossal. For instance, even the smallest branch crossing would usually have several cast-iron signs on the gates instructing passers-by to shut the gates and warning people not to trespass on the railway. Such notices are now collector's items, as are many other once-familiar items from the railways in steam days.

1. The Shed Environment

Photography at locomotive depots offered numerous possibilities as engines were moved around. Turntables, coaling plants and ash pits all added an interesting background. When all the necessary work had been completed you would often find engines in good photographic positions as they awaited their next turn of duty.

At all the larger depots the shed pilot was kept busy marshalling locomotives in order to avoid unnecessary movements. Some might be preparing to go off shed, while others were due for a boiler washout, inspection or lighting up after a period of inactivity. Depending on the location the pilot might well tow out as many as six or seven engines from the back of a shed. This was a golden opportunity for photographers as some of these engines would almost certainly end up back in the depths of the shed.

As mentioned previously, four of the regions used to grant visitor permits to individuals, and this was ideal as it allowed enough time to photograph all the engines that were in good positions, as well as giving you the chance to wait for movements around the depot. Organised visits to the Eastern and North Eastern regions meant you had to work quickly in order to keep up with the group, and in many cases you did not have time to go into the shed itself.

New steam locomotive construction went on into the early 1960s, and although increasing numbers of diesels were being built no one thought that in just a few years steam would be finished. It was astonishing just how quickly the steam locomotive shed became part of our railway history.

In the early 1950s Chester depot was home to a number of 4–4–0s with others working in daily. 2P no. 40629 was a visitor from Rhyl. The Chester engines worked local services on the North Wales line and to Crewe.

10.8.52

Only on rare occasions did one get the chance to photograph a locomotive fresh from works overhaul. No. 41945, not in steam, was inside Plaistow shed but was towed outside for the benefit of the photographers during an organised visit. No doubt it was this engine's last general overhaul, and it would not have remained in this pristine condition for long. It was withdrawn in 1959.
6.3.55

Several of these 4F 0–6–0s were fitted with ATC equipment for use on LTS lines, as in this case with no. 44348 seen here at Devons Road depot. Built in 1927, it remained in service until July 1964.

6.3.55

Work for the remaining ex-Midland Railway 1P 0–4–4Ts was becoming scarce. No. 58062, seen here at Devons Road depot, was one of those fitted for push-pull working. It was allocated to Plaistow depot which belonged to the Eastern Region. The class was introduced in 1881 and later rebuilt with a Belpaire boiler.

6.3.55

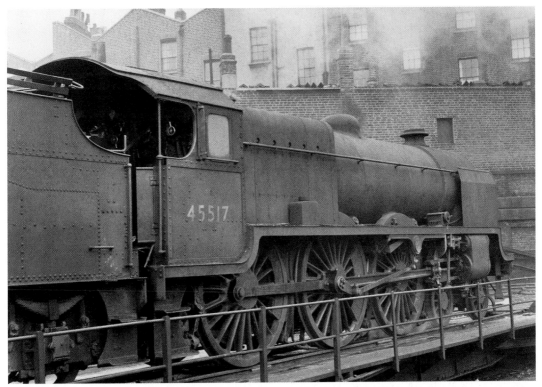

Most of the un-rebuilt 'Patriots' working into London arrived with parcel trains or specials. No. 45517, seen here turning at a smoky Camden shed, was one of those not named.

13.11.55

This photograph of the nameplate of no. 46100 *Royal Scot* was taken while the locomotive was still in service. The small lettering, heavily coated with grime, reads: 'Prior to conversion this locomotive with the Royal Scot train was exhibited at the Century of Progress Exhibition, Chicago, 1933, and made a tour of the Dominion of Canada and the United States of America. The engine and train covered 11,194 miles over the railroads of the North American continent and was inspected by 3,021,401 people. W. Gilbertson – Driver, J. Jackson – Fireman, T. Blackett – Fireman, W.C. Woods – Fitter.'

9.9.51

Fresh from Devons Road works, 3F no. 43244 stands ready to work back to Kettering, its home depot. Devons Road depot came within the Willesden district.

6.3.55

Restricted entrances were to be found at many ex-Midland Railway depots, as illustrated here by 8F no. 48024 at Wellingborough. Attention was always paid to painting white areas on the walls to remind drivers of this hazard. Wellingborough shed closed in 1966.

17.1.65

Wellingborough roundhouse was a shadow of its former self when this picture was taken. Two 8Fs, nos 48467 and 48699, and class 5 no. 45045 were present, together with examples of diesel power.
17.10.65

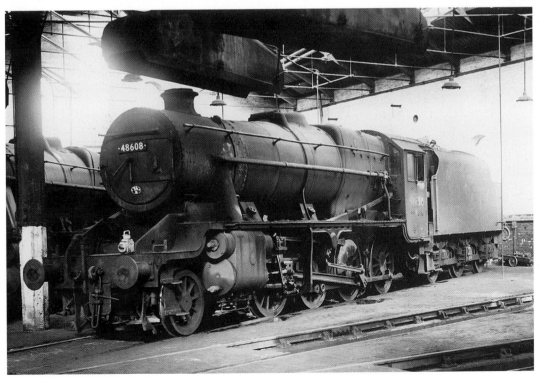

Many visitors still flocked to Wellingborough in 1965. Inside the shed is 8F no. 48608, a Mirfield engine, this former London Midland Region shed having been transferred to the North Eastern Region.
17.10.65

Class 9F 2–10–0s were still to be seen at Wellingborough until the shed finally closed. The massive outline of no. 92073 can be seen here. Note the flangeless middle set of driving wheels.

17.10.65

Typical of the condition of many steam locomotives in the mid-1960s, this is Standard 9F no. 92122 pictured at Wellingborough covered in grime, oil and grease, so much so that even after someone had rubbed over the number it was not readily visible. Some of these powerful locomotives had only short working lives in the headlong rush to change over to diesel power.

17.10.65

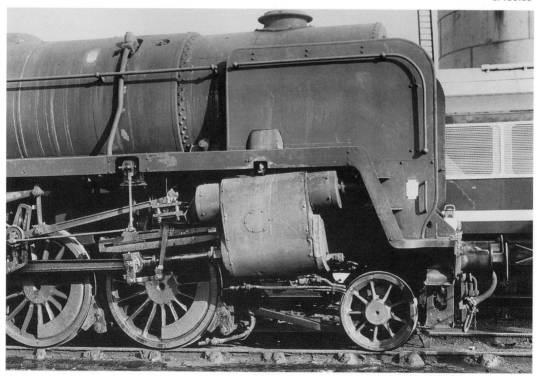

This picture of the front end of Standard class 9 2–10–0 no. 92122 reveals the clean lines and well-proportioned design of these powerful locomotives. This is a typical example of those that ran with single chimneys; others had a double chimney. By this time Wellingborough shed already had a considerable number of diesels present, one of which can be seen in the background.

17.10.65

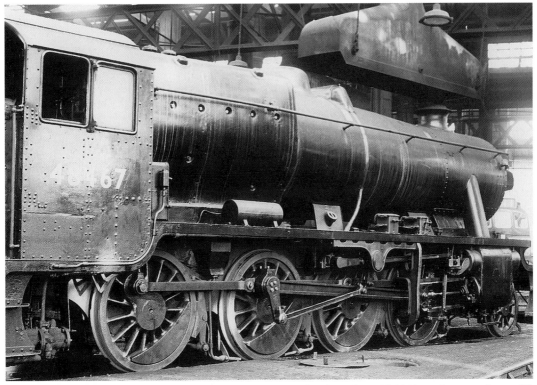

A few steam locomotives were still receiving general overhauls in the mid-1960s and one such was 8F no. 48467, seen here inside Wellingborough shed. It was to remain in service for another two and a half years, being withdrawn in June 1968.

26.12.65

Standard class 2MT no. 84005 undergoing repairs to its boiler tubes in Wellingborough shed. The numbers of steam engines here were reducing rapidly at this time, and the shed and yard had examples of many diesel types present.

8.11.64

The British Railways Standard 2MT was a development of the Ivatt design introduced in 1946. No. 84006 was photographed at Wellingborough depot. Thirty of these engines were built, all of them fitted for push-pull working.

25.4.65

Opposite: The ten Standard class 9F 2–10–0s with Franco-Crosti boilers were built in 1955 at Crewe works. It was expected that these engines would show a considerable coal saving but the design failed to live up to expectations and most went into store after just three years owing to their high maintenance requirements and corrosion. Rebuilding of the Crosti 9Fs commenced in 1959, retaining the smaller boiler and firebox but with normal draughting arrangements. No. 92026 was one year old when these pictures, showing both sides of the engine, were taken at Wellingborough.

22.7.56

Although the smokebox of 8F no. 48133 had recently received a coat of paint, signs of old paint and corrosion were still visible. This 8F was one of several allocated to Kettering, shedcode 15B, and was used principally on iron ore traffic.

11.4.53

Cab details of 8F no. 48133 can be seen in this picture. The power classification 8F was also marked on the cabside and is just visible through the grime above the locomotive's number. The 8Fs were the standard goods engines of the LMS, sturdy, powerful and well-liked by enginemen.

11.4.53

This powerful 0–10–0, no. 58100, spent thirty-seven years blasting up the famous Lickey incline, banking both passenger and heavy freight trains. Photographed at Bromsgrove on a Sunday morning, its next duty was assisting a class 5 heading a Bristol to Birmingham service. The large headlamp was fitted to the engine to help when approaching a train in the dark. This picture was taken in its last full year of service.

17.7.55

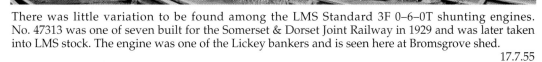

There was little variation to be found among the LMS Standard 3F 0–6–0T shunting engines. No. 47313 was one of seven built for the Somerset & Dorset Joint Railway in 1929 and was later taken into LMS stock. The engine was one of the Lickey bankers and is seen here at Bromsgrove shed.

17.7.55

Among the sizeable stud of ex-LNWR 0–8–0s to be found at Bletchley was no. 48898, which was fitted with a tender cab, clearly visible in this picture. This locomotive had a long history. Built in 1901 as a B class 0–8–0, it was converted in 1907 to an F class 2–8–0, in 1923 to a G1 class 0–8–0 and again in 1942 to a G2A. In the background is the tall signal that stood at the north end of Bletchley station.

29.4.54

Opposite, top: The prototype Ivatt 2MT no. 46400 was allocated new to Kettering depot and was soon followed by nos 46401 to 46404. In due course several others arrived, plus two of the Standard 2MTs, nos 78020 and 78021. Prior to the arrival of the Ivatt design elderly ex-Midland Railway 0–6–0s had worked the Cambridge services. The 2MTs remained at Kettering until the Cambridge line closed in 1959. No. 46400 was photographed on shed ready for its next duty.

31.5.52

Opposite, bottom: The Ivatt 2–6–0s would only just fit on the small turntable at Huntingdon East sub-shed. The turntable was only used once a day, on weekdays only, and considerable effort was required by the enginemen to operate it. No. 46496 had arrived to act as pilot for the fruit train.

17.6.52

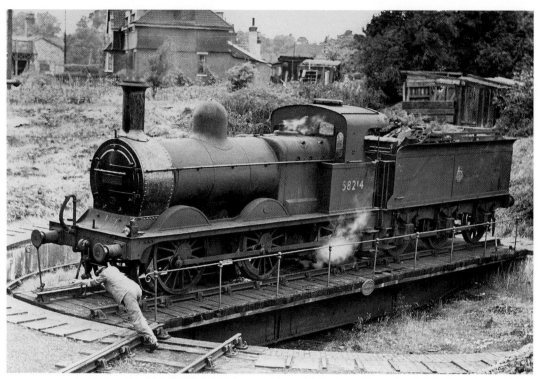

With the arrival of the Ivatt 2MT 2–6–0s at Kettering the veteran ex-Midland Railway 2F 0–6–0s soon found themselves relegated to goods working. No. 58214 is on the turntable at Huntingdon East sub-shed before working a goods back to Kettering.

6.52

Bedford shed was typical of many of the London Midland Region sheds, and its allocation in the 1950s was around forty engines. These included several 3F 0–6–0s which were widely used at the surrounding brickworks. No. 43785 was allocated to the shed for a number of years.

11.9.54

For many years 3F 0–6–0 no. 43766 was allocated to Bedford depot, spending much of its time shunting at the nearby brickworks and on trip working. It was among the last of the 3F 0–6–0s at the depot. When this picture was taken it was being stored, although its tender had been coaled so the locomotive could have quickly been returned to service. Sadly, as with so many stored engines, it was condemned and never worked again.

6.9.62

Increasing numbers of Ivatt 2MT 2–6–0s arriving at Kettering resulted in the ex-Midland Railway 2F 0–6–0s being placed in store. Three of them, headed by no. 58164, are seen here in a siding at the back of the shed. All had pieces of tarpaulin tied over their chimneys. No. 58164 had at some stage received works attention, as the smokebox and chimney had been repainted. The locomotive carried its British Railway number and front numberplate, although the tender was still lettered LMS.

31.5.52

Only one ex-Midland Railway 2F 0–6–0 was allocated to Bedford shed. No. 58241 was fitted with one of the earlier cabs that required protection for the enginemen, especially if working tender first. A tarpaulin was provided for this purpose, which can be seen hanging at the side of the tender.

23.2.52

Opposite, top: Many of the duties formerly worked by the Compounds allocated to Bedford depot had already been taken over by Standard class 4MT 4–6–0s and 4MT 2–6–4Ts. No. 41049 was among the last of the Compounds working from the depot. Although withdrawals of the class were heavy in the mid-1950s, some examples remained in service until March 1959.

11.9.54

Opposite, bottom: During the 1950s Bedford had just one 8F, no. 48177, in its allocation. In the background is a typical shed scene of the 1950s, with engines being serviced and moved into the right position for their next turn of duty.

21.8.54

Typical of many locomotive depots in the 1950s, this is the disposal point at Bedford where fires were cleaned out before coal and water supplies were topped up. In the background is a coaling plant with reserve supplies nearby. Lighting was poor and was mostly provided by gas lamps. No. 41054 was one of the depot's Compounds, mainly used on London services. 21.8.54

Several of the ex-Midland Railway 3F 0–6–0Ts were fitted with condensing apparatus for working in the London area, especially on the Metropolitan lines. No. 47223 had been transferred to Bedford. This class was introduced in 1899 and was rebuilt with Belpaire boilers, and the type was followed by the post-Grouping development known as 'Jinties'.

21.8.54

Stored locomotives were usually to be found on isolated sidings well away from the day-to-day activities of the shed. 2P 4–4–0 no. 40411 at Bedford had only wagons for company. Protection had been provided over the chimney but the tender was empty, and it is unlikely that it ever worked again.

21.8.54

The approach lines to Bedford shed, with 2MT no. 41271 leaving the depot. On the left is the coaling plant with reserve supplies. In the background are the fast lines of the main line. Signals, lamps, a water storage tank and the once very common telegraph poles complete the scene.

21.8.54

On a dull November day the fireman of push-pull-fitted 2MT no. 41271 prepares to pull the feed pipe over from the column ready to replenish the engine's water supply.

23.11.54

Class 5 no. 45253 stands under the coaling plant at Bedford. These huge concrete structures were a familiar sight at many depots. Most provided an instantly recognisable landmark.

23.1.54

The 'lion and wheel' crest can be clearly seen on the tender of 4F 0–6–0 no. 44529, as can a set of fire irons. There was some variation in the tender types fitted to 4Fs, the one here being of the high-sided type.

10.10.54

Examples of the two Standard designs stand outside Bedford shed in weak late autumn sunshine. Nearest the camera is 4MT 2–6–4T no. 80061 which was one of the locomotives that replaced the depot's Compounds. 2MT no. 84005 was used on branch services in the area.

10.10.54

The old-style cab still fitted to ex-Midland 2F 0–6–0 no. 58305 can be clearly seen in this picture. When running tender first or in bad weather conditions the enginemen would pull down and fasten the tarpaulin seen lying on the cab roof, and this offered them some protection. The coal-burning stove alongside was for use in severe weather conditions to help prevent the engine freezing up.

23.11.54

Crewe works commemorated the fact that push-pull-fitted Ivatt 2MT no. 41272 was the 7,000th engine built there by fixing a small plate on the tank side just below the emblem. This locomotive was based at Bedford before ending its working life in the West Country.
11.9.54

4F no. 43889 coaling at Burton depot. The fireman distributes the coal into various parts of the tender as it falls out of the tub. Burton was principally concerned with goods and shunting locomotives and had only a small number of passenger engines in its allocation. The most numerous class was 4F 0–6–0s which in the early 1950s comprised over half the total allocation.

10.7.53

Only a handful of these ex-LNWR 2–4–2Ts remained in service when this picture of no. 46654 was taken at Rugby. Members of this class and the 0–6–2Ts known as 'Coal Tanks' were easily recognisable by their tall chimneys. No. 46654 carried British Railways lettering on its tank sides.

5.2.53

Huge piles of coal were frequently to be seen at many locomotive depots, often spreading over a period of time to cover considerable ground space. This was the case here at Canklow depot, home to a sizeable number of 2F and 3F 0–6–0s including no. 58114, seen here on a rather gloomy summer's day.
24.5.56

Five years after nationalisation not all locomotives had received their BR number or tender lettering. Ex-LNWR 0–8–0 no. 9417 was pictured shunting at Rugby. These veterans were to be found at many London Midland Region depots during the 1950s, with a small number surviving into the early 1960s.
5.2.53

Run-down Standard class 2MT no. 78027 had almost certainly been used to tow a batch of withdrawn locomotives to Kettering on their way to Cohens scrapyard. It was photographed at the locomotive depot before returning to its home shed. These engines were basically the 1946 Ivatt design with a few alterations such as BR standard fittings.

14.3.65

Class 5 no. 45446 stands alongside the sizeable water storage tank at Rugby depot. The locomotive appears to have been on shed duties as it is coupled to wagons containing ash and clinker.

5.2.53

Wellingborough Standard 9F 2–10–0 no. 92123 had already lost its front numberplate when this picture was taken at Kettering. The depot was still open although many of the engines present were withdrawn and destined for the nearby Cohens scrapyard. Kettering closed the following year.

13.12.64

Standard 9F no. 92112, seen here at Wellingborough, was in terrible external condition, as were many steam engines in the mid-1960s. For many railwaymen the end of the days of steam could not come soon enough during the headlong rush towards dieselisation.

8.11.64

Looking at this picture one would think it was an Eastern Region depot with D16 no. 62585 and B1 no. 61302. In fact this photograph was taken at Bletchley, where Cambridge engines were daily visitors and were usually easily visible to passengers on the West Coast main-line services.

15.7.54

Ex-LNWR 0–8–0 no. 49277 turns at Bletchley. This was one of the sizeable stud of these engines allocated to the depot. Built in 1917 as a G1 class, it was rebuilt in August 1947.

15.7.54

The batch of sturdy ex-LNWR 0–8–0s at Bletchley had many duties, including the Leighton Buzzard sand trains, and occasionally they worked through to Cambridge via Bedford and Sandy. No. 49330 was photographed at its home shed ready for its next duty. This engine was completed in November 1918 and rebuilt as a G2A in January 1940.

15.7.54

Locomotives of the 0–8–0 wheel arrangement were the principal goods locomotives of the London & North Western Railway. They were powerful and reliable, and a large number were taken into LMS ownership, the majority of which were still in service on nationalisation. No. 49105 was pictured at Northampton shed in the 1950s in typically grimy condition. By this time 0–8–0s were mostly employed on short-distance goods and local workings.

5.9.54

Patriot class no. 45504 *Royal Signals* was a Crewe North engine when this picture was taken at Northampton. Most of the class spent their final years on relief and special workings and were often to be seen heading parcels and fast goods trains. No. 45504 ended its days at Bristol (Barrow Road) depot, from where it was withdrawn in March 1962.

5.9.54

Class 8F no. 48090 of Northampton depot moves off shed at Bletchley. For most of the 1950s this shed was home to a considerable number of goods engines and a sizeable stud of ex-LNWR 0–8–0s, as well as receiving visitors.

15.7.54

Standard 4MT 2–6–4T locomotives were to be found at many London Midland Region depots. No. 80066, seen here at Bletchley, was one of a small stud allocated to the depot; their various duties included working the Cambridge line services.

15.7.54

Space and facilities at Bletchley depot were limited. Here 8F no. 48656 stands near the water tanks with the coaling equipment in the background. This ex-LNWR depot received a new roof in 1953 and closed in 1965.

30.6.63

Ready for the road, this is Bletchley class 5 no. 44837. This member of the famous class was completed in September 1944 and remained in service until September 1967. Note the typically grimy condition of the engine.

9.5.65

Opposite, top: Large coal dumps were often to be seen at locomotive depots as in this picture, with even more in the row of wagons. In the background is Nottingham shed's coaling plant. 8F no. 48405 was a Mansfield engine and is seen here awaiting its return journey.

4.4.54

Opposite, bottom: Many old locomotive tenders were given a new lease of life as sludge-carriers. They were modified to carry lime deposits from water-softening plants for disposal. The one in this picture still carries the LMS lettering, and on the side are instructions to return to Nottingham depot. Alongside is 2P 4–4–0 no. 40493, leaving the shed for its next duty.

4.4.54

Coal is piled high on the tender of Compound no. 41185 as it stands ready to leave Nottingham shed. Locomotives of this class were still extensively used on semi-fast, secondary and local passenger services at this time. All this was about to change as more modern motive power became available. As a result many Compounds were placed in store or saw little use. The jib of the Nottingham breakdown crane also appears in this picture.

4.4.54

The majority of the 2F 0–6–0s were running with Deeley cabs, although some still retained the earlier Johnson design as seen here on no. 58271 at Nottingham. Extra protection for the enginemen when needed was provided by the tarpaulin sheet.

4.4.54

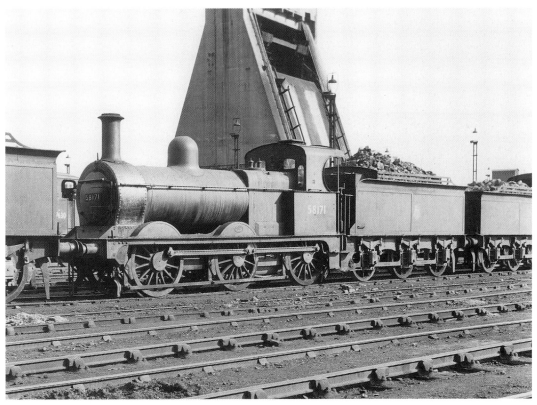

In their heyday the 2F 0–6–0s were main-line goods locomotives. The Midland Railway had a sizeable stud, a large number of which were taken into British Railways stock (albeit by this time they were mostly confined to branch-line and short-trip workings). No. 58171 stands at Toton, with the massive coaling plant in the background.

4.4.54

Workstained 2F 0–6–0 no. 58133 and a 4F stand in the yard at Toton. During the early 1950s more than ten 2F engines were to be found at this large shed, which had over 150 engines in its allocation.

4.4.54

The very useful 8F
2–8–0s were a Stanier
design introduced in
1935. During the war
years locomotives of
the class were built at
the works of the GWR,
SR and LNER, as well
as by private builders.
Many were sent
overseas during the
war, some of them
never to return. Nos
48285 and 48543 are
seen here at Toton shed.
4.4.54

It's Sunday morning at Toton shed and several of the depot's allocation of Stanier 8F 2–8–0s are at rest. The once-familiar ash pits on the left of this picture had also been cleaned out. Toton shed was well-lit even in the 1950s, and several of the lighting posts appear in this picture.

4.4.54

Fowler 4F no. 43930 was one of the successful superheated design introduced by the Midland Railway in 1911. It is seen here at its home depot Nottingham, with the coaling plant in the background. A post-Grouping development of this class was introduced by the LMS in 1924 with 580 locomotives being built.

4.4.54

The massive LMS Beyer-Garratt 2–6–6–2Ts weighed over 155 tons. All but two of the 33-strong class were fitted with revolving coal bunkers. No. 47991 was photographed at Toton shed. Completed in November 1930, it remained in service until December 1955. The class became extinct in March 1958.

4.4.54

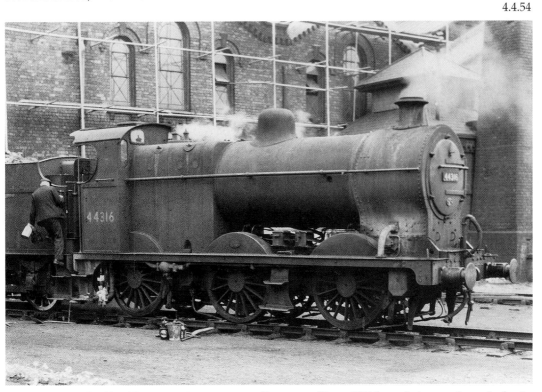

Repairs to the shed building were in progress at Burton as 4F no. 44316 was being made ready for its next duty. The 4F design was introduced in 1911 and locomotives of this class were very common in the area. In all, 772 pre- and post-Grouping 4Fs were in service.

10.7.53

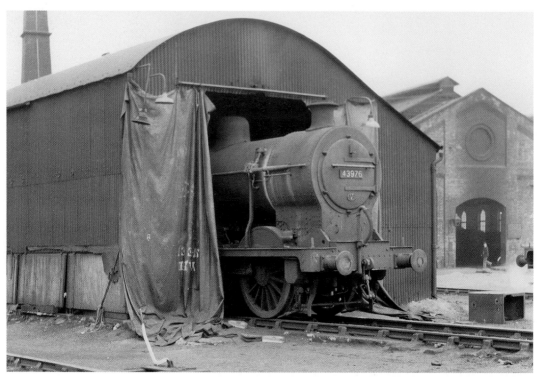

The front end of 4F no. 43976 peeps out of the inspection shed at Burton. No doors were fitted to the building and in winter large tarpaulins were pressed into service to keep out the worst of the weather. These were also used extensively during the wartime blackout.

10.7.53

Brand-new locomotives were always of interest when visiting depots adjacent to a locomotive works. Standard class 5 no. 73032 had recently been completed at Derby and was in the process of being prepared to enter service. No shedplate had yet been fitted, and the red flag on the buffer beam indicated that the engine must not be moved.

10.7.53

The first of the Ivatt 4MT 2–6–0s were turned out with huge double chimneys which were later changed to those of a conventional type. No. 43027 ran with this ugly stovepipe chimney while tests were carried out. The engine was photographed at its home shed Derby.

10.7.53

This picture shows the valve gear of 'Jubilee' class no. 45594 *Bhopal*, built in 1935. Chalked on the cylinder cover is the inscription 'Ned was here' – I wonder who Ned was and what he was doing here over forty years ago!

24.6.62

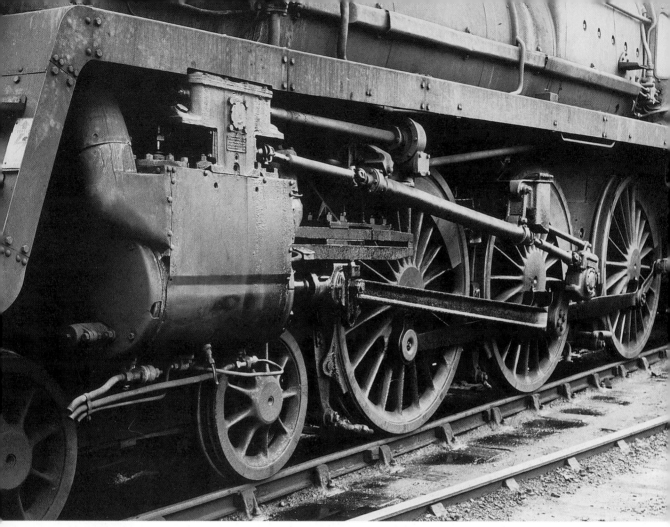

Caprotti valve gear was fitted to thirty of the British Railways Standard class 5s, nos 73125–73154. This type of valve gear required specialist knowledge and maintenance. Patricroft was to become the home shed for those working in England, but not for the ten allocated to Scottish Region depots. This picture shows the valve gear fitted to no. 73144, which was withdrawn in August 1967.

12.6.64

Opposite, top: During the early 1950s Crewe works had a fascinating selection of locomotives in use as works shunters, among them ex-LNWR 0–6–0ST no. 3323, seen here still carrying its LNWR number. Also in use was an ex-Caledonian Railway 0–4–0ST, two ex-LNWR 0–4–2Ts and several ex-LNWR 0–6–0s. Sadly no. 3323 was cut up in 1954, and its four classmates in use at Wolverton carriage works followed in the late 1950s.

12.8.52

Opposite, bottom: Two of these unusual 0–4–2STs remained active in the 1950s, both at Crewe works. The type was first introduced by F.W. Webb for the London & North Western Railway in 1896, when they were known as Bissel truck designs. No. 47862 is pictured here shunting in the works yard and carrying the W10 duty headboard. Sister engine no. 47865 was withdrawn in 1953, with no. 47862 going in 1956.

12.8.52

During the early 1950s two classes of ex-London & North Western Railway 0–6–0s were still active, albeit they were being rapidly withdrawn. The classes were the 'Coal Engines' and later 18-inch goods known as 'Cauliflowers'. No. 58426 was one of the latter. The engine, already in poor condition, had been towed to Crewe works for scrapping.

12.8.52

The first two members of the 'Patriot' class were rebuilds of the LNWR 'Claughton' class, retaining their original wheels and other parts. No. 45500 *Patriot* was photographed at Longsight ready to work back to its home depot Carlisle Upperby. In the pit underneath the engine a member of the shed staff goes about his duties.

22.9.57

'Jinty' no. 47550 standing in a siding with the Bristol (Barrow Road) depot breakdown train. Barrow Road was a former Midland Railway shed, and in the early 1950s it had nearly sixty locomotives on its books, including ten 'Jubilees'. It closed in 1965.

31.8.55

At Bristol (Barrow Road) 2MT 2–6–2T no. 41240 is acting as shed pilot while 4F no. 44272 is receiving attention. In the background a wagon can be seen on its way to the top of the coaling plant.

31.8.55

The first of Stanier's famous class 5 4–6–0s made its debut in 1934, the class eventually totalling 842 locomotives. Among them were a number of experimental engines, some with Caprotti valve gear. No. 45300, seen here at Llandudno, was typical of the class design. Completed in January 1937, it remained in traffic until December 1965.

12.7.64

Caprotti valve gear was also fitted to some of the Standard class 5s. No. 73135 was photographed at Llandudno Junction shed in deplorable external condition.

12.6.66

During the 1960s very few locomotives placed in store were ever returned to traffic. Standard class 2MT no. 84020 had received the customary sheeting over its chimney before being put out to grass at Llandudno Junction shed. These engines were a BR development of the Ivatt 2MTs introduced in 1946.

12.7.64

The ex-Lancashire & Yorkshire Railway 0–6–0s enjoyed a long association with the North Wales coast line. But time had run out for no. 52119, seen here at Llandudno Junction shed; already withdrawn, it was awaiting its last journey.

9.6.63

Llandudno Junction shed had a considerably reduced allocation when this picture was taken. Class 3F 0–6–0T no. 47669 stands alongside rebuilt 'Patriot' no. 45534 *E. Total Broadhurst*. Other engines present included Standard and Stanier class 5s. This former LNWR depot closed in 1966.

16.6.63

Standard class 4MT no. 75032, seen here at Llandudno Junction shed, had recently been used as the motive power for a special, as the train reporting number is still on the smokebox door. These powerful mixed-traffic engines were introduced in 1951 and soon replaced many older locomotives.

24.6.62

There was little variation among the Midland Compounds. One exception was no. 40933, seen here at Monument Lane shed, which from 1954 ran with a Fowler 3,500-gallon tender, rebuilt with high curved sides in 1933. This engine was withdrawn in April 1958.

22.7.56

The nameplate of 'Jubilee' class no. 45699 *Galatea*, which was completed in April 1936 and withdrawn in November 1964. Happily, this locomotive still survives – originally purchased for spares, it is now expected to be returned to steam once again.

21.7.64

In the last years of steam the cleaning of locomotives was a low priority at many depots. 'Jubilee' class no. 45567 *South Australia* was covered in a considerable amount of grease and grime when this picture was taken. Time was running out for this engine as it was withdrawn from service in January 1965.

12.7.64

The successful Ivatt 4MT 2–6–0s were still being constructed well into British Railways days, the last of the class being delivered in September 1952. No. 43122 was completed in August 1951. This front-end study was taken at Bletchley and shows clearly the high running plate, a distinctive feature of these engines. No. 43122 was withdrawn from service in March 1967.

9.5.65

Sunshine and shade combine to produce this dramatic picture of Ivatt 4MT no. 43135 at Skipton depot. Built after nationalisation, this engine was in service for just fifteen years.

20.9.64

In the mid-1960s most depots had numerous steam locomotives standing in the yards. Carlisle Upperby was no exception. 'Royal Scot' no. 46118 *Royal Welsh Fusilier* had already lost its nameplates, although surprisingly the smokebox numberplate was still in situ. After four months in storage it was towed north of the border for scrapping.

18.9.64

'Princess Coronation' class no. 46250 *City of Lichfield* was completed in May 1944. It was stored at Carlisle Upperby depot after being withdrawn in September 1964 and ended its days in a Troon scrapyard.

18.9.64

The nameplate and crest of rebuilt 'Patriot' class no. 45526 *Morecambe and Heysham* was still on the locomotive at Carlisle Upperby although it had been withdrawn from service.

18.9.64

One class to be found at a great many London Midland Region depots was the 3F 0–6–0. The small-engine policy of the Midland Railway relied heavily on the 0–6–0 wheel arrangement. In their heyday these engines were responsible for much of the goods traffic. By the 1950s most of their work was on local goods and short-trip workings. No. 43595 was one of a number based at Royston shed.

24.6.56

The Fowler 7F 0–8–0s were developed from the very reliable and sturdy LNWR G2 class. In all, 175 were constructed over a three-year period, the first making its debut in March 1929. As a class they were generally not as successful as the LNWR engines. In the 1950s all were concentrated in the north-west. No. 49560, seen here at Bolton, was nearing the end of its days as just three months later it was withdrawn.

22.9.57

Although developed from the well-known LNWR 0–8–0s, the 175 Fowler engines introduced in 1929 were not as popular at some depots. Withdrawals commenced in 1949, with a considerable number being cut up between 1949 and 1951. No. 49532, seen here inside Bolton shed, remained in service until May 1956. The class became extinct in 1961.

16.10.55

The shed pilot's duties included moving wagons as required to the coaling plant and marshalling engines ready for their next duty. Many veterans ended their working days on such duties. This ex-Midland Railway 0–6–0T no. 41661 was on shed pilot duty at Stourton. Although it had been rebuilt with a Belpaire boiler, it still retained the open cab.

13.5.56

A familiar sight at steam depots were the wagons used to transport away the large amounts of ash and clinker produced. Trafford Park was very tidy, and the shed staff had done a fine job. It was very different at some sheds, with piles of ash left lying around. Someone had recently cleaned out the smokebox of Standard 4MT no. 42469, as little heaps of ash can be seen on the running plate.

16.10.55

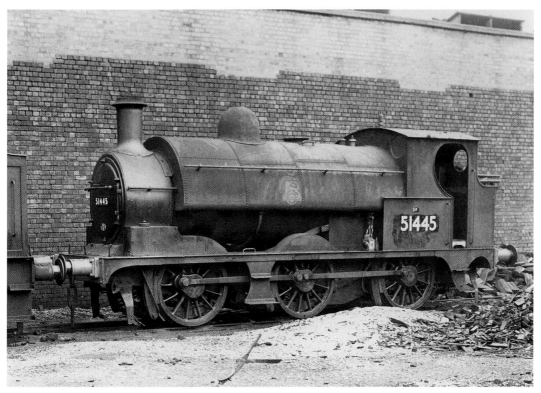

The ex-Lancashire & Yorkshire Railway 0–6–0STs were rebuilds of an 0–6–0 design first introduced by Barton Wright in 1876. Rebuilding commenced in 1891. During the 1950s examples were to be found at numerous depots in the north-west. No. 51445 is seen here at Bolton.

22.9.57

It was not unusual to see locomotives in service showing signs of external damage, as was the case with 0–6–0ST no. 51408 at Bolton, which has a large dent in the saddle tank. These engines were the basic shunters in the north-west, sharing the duties with the well-known 3F 0–6–0Ts known as 'Jinties'.

22.9.57

The driver of 3F no. 43183 checks round his engine before leaving Normanton. This locomotive was one of the small batch with 4ft 11in driving wheels which had been rebuilt with larger class 3 Belpaire boilers.
13.5.56

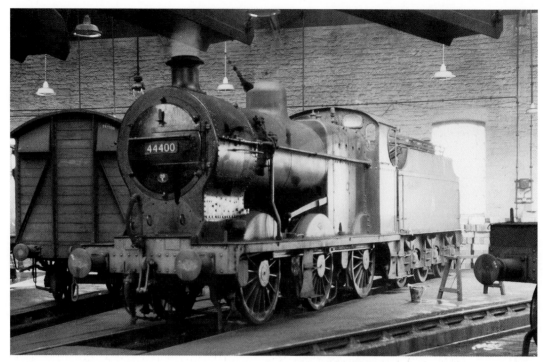

Many of the Midland Railway depots were 'roundhouses', as was the case at Bradford Manningham where this picture of 4F 0–6–0 no. 44400 was taken. This engine, built in 1927, remained in service until October 1965.

13.5.56

Two ex-Midland Railway 3F 0–6–0s, both in light steam, await their next duty in the confines of Manningham shed. No. 43553 and no. 43784 were typical of well over three hundred locomotives of this type to be found in service in the mid-1950s.

13.5.56

The diminutive 1ft 6in 0–4–0ST *Wren*, works no. 2825, was built in 1887 by Beyer Peacock for the Horwich works internal system. Boiler pressure was 170lb per sq. in with 5in x 6in outside cylinders and Joy valve gear. The name can be seen on the large dome. Fortunately, this interesting little engine has survived into preservation.

22.9.57

Many of the Johnson 0–4–4Ts introduced by the Midland Railway in 1881 were fitted for push-pull working. No. 58066, photographed at Royston shed, was among those rebuilt with a Belpaire boiler. Only a few were still in service in the mid-1950s.

24.6.56

In the 1950s quite a number of ex-Midland Railway 3F 0–6–0s had been placed in store at various depots. Among them was no. 43705, seen here at Royston depot with the customary tarpaulin sheeting over the chimney. These engines were rebuilt with Belpaire boilers during their long service.

24.6.56

The arrival of the Ivatt 2MT 2–6–2Ts and later Standard designs resulted in many older tank locomotives becoming surplus to requirements. No. 50752 at Sowerby Bridge was an example of the ex-Lancashire & Yorkshire Railway 2P 2–4–2Ts with 2-ton coal capacity. Some members of the class were rebuilt with Belpaire boilers, longer tanks and extended coal bunkers.

15.5.56

The original ex-Lancashire & Yorkshire Railway 2–4–2Ts were limited by the amount of coal and water they could carry. In 1898 the first engines with longer tanks and a 4-ton capacity coal bunker (double that of the earlier examples) appeared. No. 50865, seen here at Huddersfield, was one of these.

13.5.56

Class 5 no. 44927, carrying a train reporting number, reverses gently on to the turntable at Low Moor shed. This was an ex-Lancashire & Yorkshire Railway shed which, during the 1950s, had an allocation of almost forty locomotives.

13.5.56

Class 5s were still being turned out in early British Railways days. Among them was no. 44732, completed in February 1949. It is seen here taking water at Farnley Junction. This locomotive remained in service until July 1967.

13.5.56

The first design of the Fowler 4MT 2–6–4Ts introduced in 1927 did not have side-window cabs, as seen in this picture of no. 42410 at Wakefield shed. The first of the side-window cab engines was introduced in 1933, with thirty built during that year. The last examples in 1934 were followed by Stanier's own 2–6–4T design.

13.5.56

This side view of Stanier 4MT 2–6–4T no. 42664 at Low Moor shed shows clearly the cab details. Construction of this class went on until 1943, and was followed by the Fairburn 2–6–4Ts, the first of these being completed in 1945. No. 42664 was turned out in July 1942 and remained in service until November 1966.

20.3.66

Many 'Britannias' ended their working days in the north-west, some after periods in store in other regions. No. 70016 *Ariel* had worked into Leeds Holbeck from its home shed Carlisle. The engine was typical of the poor external conditions of most of the class at this time, having already lost its nameplates. Diesel power was very much in evidence, as can be seen from the 'Peak' on the same siding.

20.3.66

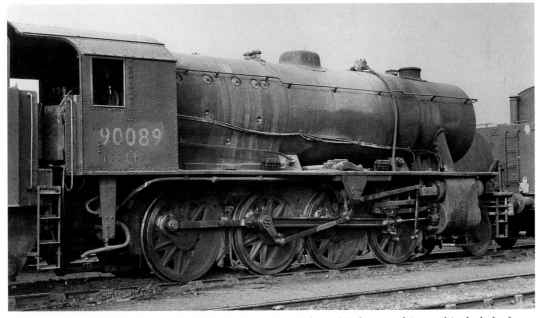

Wakefield was the principal shed of the 25 district throughout BR days, and its stud included a large number of WD 2–8–0s, which were mostly used on coal traffic. In 1965 the allocation of these engines reached sixty, including workstained no. 90089, seen here at its home shed. Originally a Lancashire & Yorkshire Railway depot, Wakefield was transferred from the London Midland Region to the North Eastern Region in 1956.

20.3.66

Standard class 9F no. 92006 awaits its return working at Normanton shed. The engine had lost its shedplate and someone has painted it on; note also the word York on the buffer beam. It was the practice in LNER days to put the engine's allocation there. The front numberplate has had its background painted rather than the numbers being picked out as was usual. Many of these fine locomotives had short working lives before making their last journey.

20.3.66

By the mid-1950s many of the remaining steam locomotives had lost front number- and shedplates, the latter having gone from 9F no. 92205, seen here at Wakefield. Many of the named engines lost their nameplates at this time. Steam had already finished completely in many parts of the country.

20.3.66

2. Under Repair

One of the commonest reasons for steam locomotive failure was a bearing running hot, and as a result it was not unusual to find engines with wheel-sets removed while the offending parts were given a new lease of life. Lack of space was frequently a problem so the engines would be towed outside and left in a siding until their turn came to be returned to traffic. As a result some very strange sights greeted visitors.

The limited repair facilities and fitters available at many sheds could often result in locomotives having to wait their turn, especially if there had been a bad patch with several failures around the same time. Working on steam engines was heavy, dirty work, especially in the final years when oil and grime were commonplace.

Compounds were very much in evidence at Derby during the early 1950s. No. 41154, seen here receiving attention from a fitter, was a Trafford Park engine. Two other members of the class can also be seen in this picture, taken on a dismal summer's day.

10.7.53

At many depots space in repair shops and bays was limited and locomotives under repair would often be moved outside until work could be completed. Here Compound no. 41062 waits outside Sheffield minus its middle wheel-set. Built in 1924, it remained in service until May 1959.

24.6.56

The weight of the front end of Compound no. 41105 was supported by the Rugby breakdown crane prior to the refitting of the front bogie. Additional support was provided by a pile of wooden blocks under the buffer beam.

5.2.53

'Princess Coronation' class no. 46242 *City of Glasgow* under repair in the yard at Willesden depot, its front end supported by a sleeper and blocks. Just over a year later this engine was involved in the Harrow crash when working the Perth–London sleeping car service.

9.9.51

It was not uncommon to find failed locomotives dumped in the shed yard until repairs could be completed. This Ivatt 2–6–0, no. 46502, is awaiting the return of its pony truck. Just two years old at the time, it remained in service until February 1967.

4.4.54

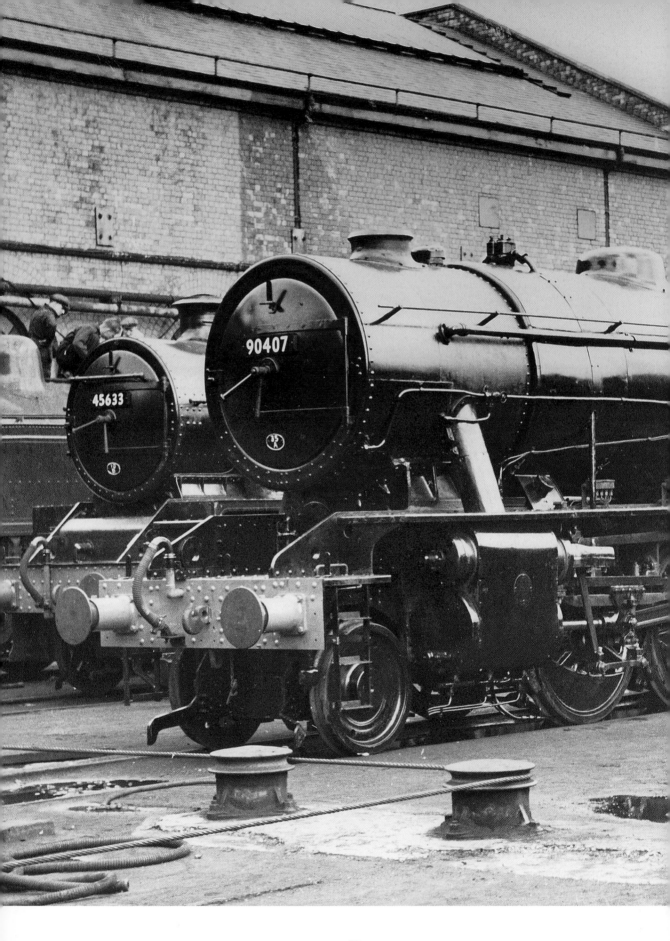

Two WD 2–8–0s fresh from general overhaul at Crewe works wait to be reunited with their tenders. No. 90407 was a New England engine. In the background, also fresh from works, is 'Jubilee' class no. 45633 *Aden* from Preston depot. 12.8.52

Although it was only recently ex-works, Class 5 no. 44755 had run into trouble and was undergoing repairs at Crewe North depot. One of the Caprotti valve gear engines, it was also fitted with Timken roller bearings and a double chimney. Built in 1945 and delivered shortly after nationalisation, it remained in service until October 1964.

12.8.52

Crewe North had several un-rebuilt 'Patriot' class engines in its allocation, including no. 45507 *Royal Tank Corps*, seen here awaiting attention to its front bogie. Members of the class were widely used on specials, excursion trains and also parcels and fast freight workings. No. 45507 was withdrawn in October 1962 and after several months in store was cut up at Horwich works.

12.8.52

'Princess Coronation' class no. 46245 *City of London* was in a very sorry state when photographed in Crewe works yard. Only one pair of driving wheels, the front bogie and the trailing wheels were present. Beyond it is a set of frames of an unidentified 4–6–0 minus boiler and cab and with all the pipework lying loose on the frames.

12.8.52

The cab fittings being replaced on Class 5 no. 45250 after the engine had received a general overhaul at Crewe works. The rest of the locomotive had already been repainted; only the cab remained to be done. The number and the power classification above it had already been replaced, leaving just the surrounding area for repainting when all the chalked messages had been dealt with.

12.8.52

Two class 5s fresh from Crewe works receive final attention in the yard. No. 45406, nearest the camera, is waiting to be transferred to the paint shop for a complete repaint. No. 44920 in the background had already been repainted.

12.8.52

Opposite, top: Class 4F no. 44447 had been 'stopped' at Bletchley for minor repairs. Note the rather battered bench complete with vices and also the steel wagon behind the engine which almost certainly would have remained there for some considerable time.

15.7.54

Opposite, bottom: One of Bletchley depot's trusty 8F 2–8–0s, no. 48493, stands inside the shed prior to examination. In 1965 over half of the depot's allocation consisted of 8Fs, with seventeen on its books.

9.5.58

The repair bay at Bletchley depot was limited and here 'Royal Scot' no. 46120 takes up most of the space available. The engine was in lamentable condition at this time. Allocated to Crewe, it is unlikely to have done much, if any, work again as it was condemned in July 1963. After two months in store at Crewe works it was cut up there.

30.6.63

(*Opposite, top*) Locomotive failures on the West Coast main line anywhere in the vicinity of Bletchley were usually towed to the shed for attention. A few limped in under their own power. 'Royal Scot' class no. 46120 *Royal Inniskilling Fusilier* had been examined by a fitter although no repairs had been started when this picture was taken.

30.6.63

(*Opposite, bottom*) Although the repair facilities at Bletchley were limited there was a fairly constant stream of work provided by failures on the main line. 'Royal Scot' class no. 46111 *Royal Fusilier* was a Longsight engine. Protruding from the engine's cab is a 'not to be moved' sign'.

5.8.54

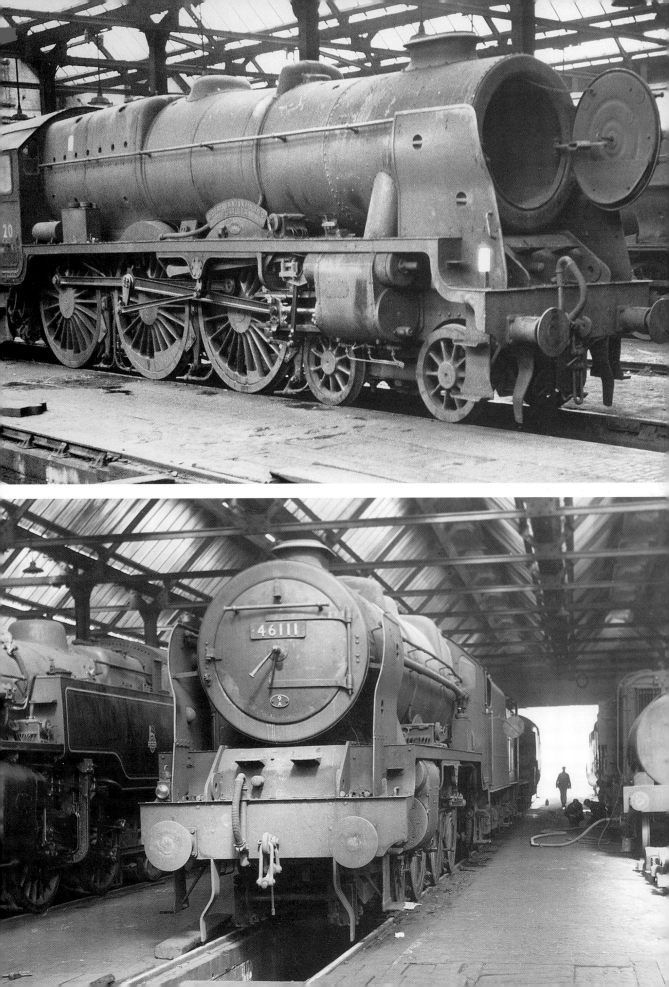

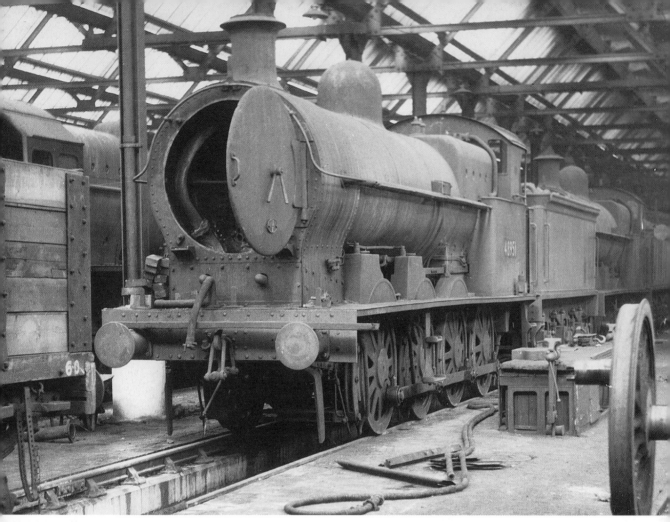

The ex-LNWR 0–8–0s had only minor differences in British Railways days but some had a long history behind them. No. 48951, seen here under repair at Bletchley, started life in August 1904 as a B class 4-cylinder 'Compound' 0–8–0 with outside cylinders and was rebuilt as a G1 class in October 1923. These locomotives carried a shedplate on the smokebox door but no front numberplate.

27.2.55

Opposite, top: Another casualty under repair at Bletchley. 'Jubilee' class no. 45737 *Atlas* was a Bushberry engine. In the foreground can be seen a fitter's bench, some welding equipment and a collection of miscellaneous bits and pieces, with another workbench next to the engine.

5.8.54

Opposite, bottom: Push-pull-fitted Standard 2MT no. 84002 stands in the repair bay at Bletchley. These engines were a development of the highly regarded Ivatt design introduced in 1946.

9.5.65

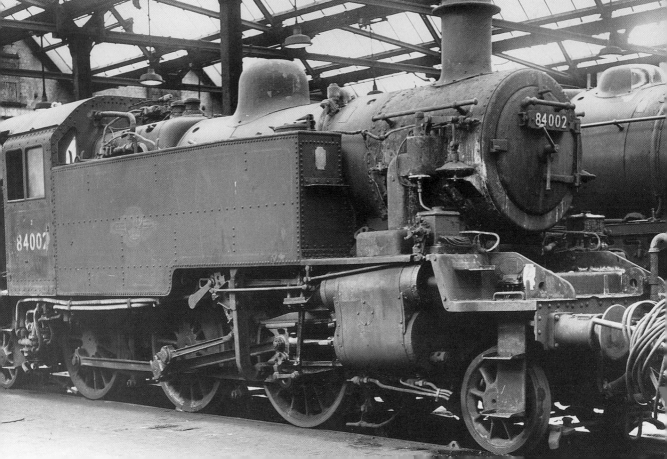

This was a rare sight at Bletchley. This is WD 2–8–0 no. 90136, an Eastern Region engine allocated to 38A Colwick depot in Nottingham. Having run into trouble, it had been taken to Bletchley for repairs. The coupling rods and valve had been dismantled.

29.4.56

One of Bletchley's 'Jinties', no. 47521, stands next to the repair bay. These were the standard LMS shunting locomotives and were to be found throughout the London Midland Region. Some were allocated to sheds formerly in LMS territory which had changed regions.

21.8.54

3. On the Move

When steam provided the principal motive power there was always the temptation not to photograph trains headed by locomotives of the most numerous classes, especially if they were not named. On the London Midland Region several types fell within this category, including the 3F 0–6–0Ts known as 'Jinties', the standard LMS shunting tank, and also the 4F 0–6–0s which were to be found at the majority of depots. Two designs by William Stanier also tended to be overlooked. These were the ubiquitous class 5s and the true workhorses of the region, the 8F 2–8–0s.

The focus was very much on the express passenger engines, and on unusual and older types that still remained in service. When possible, I always took the attitude that irrespective of what type of locomotive was heading a train I would photograph it if the location and weather conditions were suitable.

Beyer-Garratt 2–6–6–2T no. 47962 running bunker first heads a heavy coal train through Bedford Midland Road station. These locomotives were still a familiar sight on the Midland main line in the early 1950s. Withdrawals commenced in 1955 and in March 1958 the class became extinct.

23.6.54

Gas lamps, station trolleys and barrows can be seen on the station platform at Bedford Midland Road as the Beyer-Garratt running on clear signals ambles through with its heavy coal train. Most goods came through the station. The fast lines cannot be seen in this picture as they were over to the right.

23.6.54

Beyer-Garratt 2–6–6–2T no. 47980 takes water at Kettering on its journey north with a heavy iron ore train. Introduced in 1937 with fixed coal bunkers, most of the 33-strong class were later fitted with revolving coal bunkers, as seen here.

11.4.53

In 1932 Stanier introduced these 0–4–4Ts fitted for push-pull working, but only ten were built. No. 41902 is seen here on pilot duties at Bletchley carrying out its work with both goods and passenger stock. No. 41902 and eight other members of the class were withdrawn in 1959, leaving just one to survive into the 1960s.

29.4.56

Ivatt 4MT no. 43045 working hard with a 'special' passing Bletchley no. 2 signal-box. The 4MT design was to prove itself soon after its introduction in 1947. The high running plate and huge double chimney fitted to the first examples aroused much comment.

29.4.56

Sandy station with Standard 4MT no. 80083 heading a Bletchley to Cambridge service which included a horsebox, not an unusual sight at this time. The LMR station here was situated alongside the Eastern Region station, and access to both was by the footbridge.

31.7.54

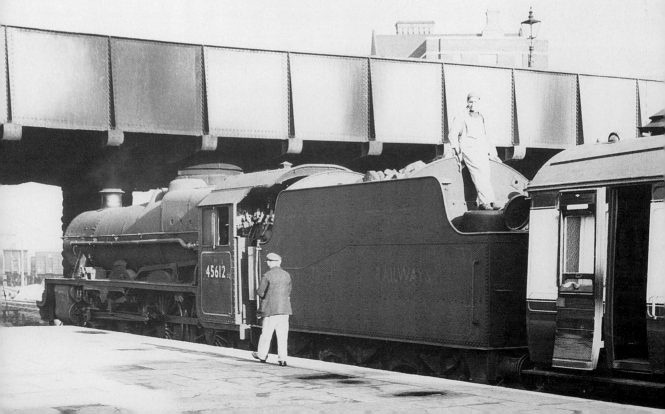

The station at Huntingdon East has long since disappeared, and its former site is now occupied by a car park for the main-line station. Other items of interest are the footbridge with its sign and gas lighting, and the check rail on the left-hand track, the station being on a sharp curve. No. 46496 was waiting to pilot the evening fruit train on its journey to Kettering.

17.6.52

Opposite, top: The LMR line from Bletchley to Cambridge was a useful cross-country route for both passenger and goods traffic. Here 8F no. 48549 starts the climb from Sandy station to cross over the East Coast main line on its journey home. Now, after all these years, plans exist to restore this cross-country route, although it will require re-routing around Sandy.

31.7.54

Opposite, bottom: The fireman of 'Jubilee' class no. 45612 *Jamaica* takes the opportunity of a brief rest as the tender refills with water. The locomotive, still lettered British Railways on the tender, was heading a St Pancras express at Leicester.

3.11.51

Typical of many cross-country services that still existed in the 1950s, here Ivatt 2MT 2–6–0 no. 46404 leaves Huntingdon East with the afternoon train to Cambridge. It was still on LMR territory, which extended as far as Godmanchester. This route was among those closed in the Beeching cuts.

16.3.54

Locomotives taking on water was a familiar sight in steam days. Ivatt 2–6–0 no. 46496 was photographed at Huntingdon East at the old GN and GE joint platforms. Note also the water crane with its attendant heating stove, and the footbridge.

17.6.52

Huntingdon no. 1 signal-box controlled both the East Coast main line and the Kettering branch. Here Ivatt 2MT no. 46496 has just arrived at Huntingdon East with the afternoon service to Cambridge and is exchanging the token with the signalman. Note the rather unusual signal, the concrete post having signal arms for both directions.

8.3.55

'Royal Scot' no. 46134 *The Cheshire Regiment* rattles through Rugby heading a long parcel train. Nearest the locomotive are several four-wheeled vehicles, including a container on a flat wagon.

29.5.54

The versatile Hughes-designed 5MT locomotives, widely known as 'Crabs', were used on numerous duties ranging from local passenger excursions to parcels and freight. Here two members of the class are pictured at Rugby. No. 42813 of Nuneaton is nearest the camera, with no. 42840 in the background.

5.2.53

Class 5 no. 45373 was busy at Skipton depot moving engines around ready for their next duty. Shrouded with steam, it was caught by the camera during a short lull in the proceedings. No. 45373 completed thirty years' service; built in 1937, it was withdrawn in September 1967.

20.9.64

Several Ivatt 2MT 2–6–2Ts were allocated to Bedford in the 1950s, and most were fitted for push-pull working. Their duties included the Northampton and Hitchin line trains. No. 41329, seen here at Bedford Midland Road station on carriage duties, was the last of the class built, being completed in May 1952, well after nationalisation. It had only a short working life as it was withdrawn in June 1964. This successful class was continued with the 84XXX series of Standard designs with a few modifications.

23.6.54

Opposite, top: Class 5 no. 44753 at Saltley. This engine was one of the batch that had Timken roller bearings as well as Caprotti valve gear. Completed in March 1948, it remained in service until July 1965.

22.7.56

Opposite, bottom: Class 4F no. 44332 stops to take on water on the main line at Bedford while heading a mixed freight. The fireman is struggling to get the heavy supply pipe into the right place.

21.8.54

Steam was still very much in control when this picture of no. 10100 was taken at Kettering. This locomotive was designed by Ivatt & Fell, and was a 4–8–4 diesel mechanical design powered by four 500hp 12-cylinder engines. On the left of this picture an 8F 2–8–0 heads north with a heavy iron ore train.

3.5.52

Opposite, top: Class 2P 4–4–0 no. 40485 had just arrived at Peterborough East with a train from Leicester. Trains from Rugby and Northampton also used this station. Peterborough East closed to passengers in 1966 but was used as a parcels centre for some time afterwards.

5.2.53

Opposite, bottom: Patriot class no. 45515 *Caernarvon* had arrived at Rugby with a stock train. Engines of this type were often seen on these duties and also on specials and excursion traffic. No. 45515 was completed in October 1932 and withdrawn in June 1962.

5.2.53

The LMS 2–6–4Ts were mainly used on secondary and cross-country services, as were the later British Railways class 4 2–6–4Ts. Stanier 2cyl. no. 42446 stands ready to leave a bay platform at Rugby. The engine was completed in June 1936 and remained in service until April 1964.

29.5.54

4. Rolling Stock Miscellany

One thing I always regret is that I did not take more pictures of the fascinating collection of rolling stock still around in the 1950s and 1960s. Old coaches of pre-Grouping origin were commonplace, with even older examples ending their days in departmental use. Wagons existed for just about every possible type of load that could travel by rail. Visit almost any locomotive shed, shunting yard or departmental depot and you would be sure to find something of interest. After withdrawal, locomotive tenders could be given a second lease of life as sludge- or water-carriers.

In those days any accident or lifting requirement would see the breakdown cranes based at principal depots called into action. Within a short time a locomotive was commandeered and a crew assembled from shed staff, and the train was under way, in an emergency situation travelling under express headcodes – an interesting sight if the motive power was a WD 2–8–0. The services of two or more cranes might be called upon in some cases. In the 1960s these trains and even the steam cranes themselves were painted red. Watching one of the larger cranes preparing for a heavy lift was fascinating. Once the problem was cleared the engineering department would arrive to carry out any necessary repairs to track work and infrastructure. During the 1950s and 1960s their train would almost certainly include some old vehicles.

The Crewe South breakdown crane no. RS. 1005.50 with its jib wagon no. DM 299581 and attendant four-wheeled truck. This was a large crane as Crewe was a principal rail centre.

12.2.67

Bletchley breakdown crane no. R1025.15 with its attendant trucks and vintage six-wheel coach. The crane itself was built by Cowans & Sheldon of Carlisle, and was an early design.

15.7.54

The Llandudno Junction breakdown crane had recently changed and the previous unit seen here, Cowans & Sheldon no. 1854 built in 1893 and jib truck no. 114903, had been put out to grass. The number RS 1023.15 can be seen near the cylinder.

12.7.64

Recently moved to Llandudno Junction shed, this is Cowans & Sheldon no. 3765 RS 1008.36 built in 1917. The jib truck is no. DM 770000. Breakdown cranes were to be found at many principal depots. They were used to deal with emergencies and, on occasions, to help with engineering works.

12.7.64

The Mirfield breakdown train consisted of a 20-ton capacity crane, which can just be seen on the left, and this interesting six-wheeler no. DM 168975 (M), lettered MP Mirfield. The vehicle was 33ft long, built as a brake third *c.* 1885; it had been considerably altered by the provision of sliding doors over what were once compartments.

13.5.56

Running as part of the Llandudno breakdown crane set was this veteran six-wheel coach, no. DM 284670. Part of this vehicle was used to carry first aid equipment. Vehicles such as this were still commonplace even during the 1960s. It had started life as a passenger coach of London & North Western origin.

12.7.64

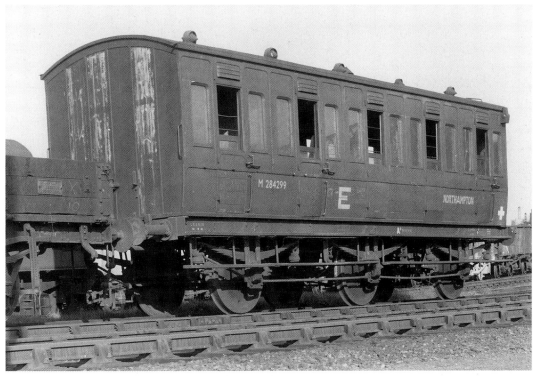

Many old carriages were to have a second lease of life in the hands of the various engineers departments. No. M 284299, a six-wheeled example, was allocated to Northampton. First aid equipment was carried, as indicated by the cross on the right. This and the example below were of London & North Western Railway origin.

5.9.54

Another six-wheeled coach to be given a second lease of life in departmental use was no. M 284604, which was part of the Bletchley breakdown train. These vehicles also carried first aid equipment, as shown by the cross at the end.

15.7.54

Throughout this period more modern rolling stock gradually replaced earlier six-wheeled coaches as breakdown vehicles. This is no. DM 395843, in red livery, at Wellingborough depot. The lettering at the far end reads MPD Wellingborough. It was converted to a staff coach in 1963, and was formerly LMS P1 BCK no. M6723M of Lot 454, built at Wolverton in 1929.

17.10.65

This tool van, no. DM 395844, was part of the Wellingborough depot breakdown crane. Painted red, it was photographed standing in the shed yard. It was formerly LMS P1 BTO no. M9844M to diagram 1693, built at Wolverton in 1927.

6.3.66

Years of exposure to the elements had resulted in the lettering LMS being visible again on tender no. 1319. Conversion into a water carrier resulted in its gaining a further lease of life. But it seems to be not in use and was perhaps awaiting scrapping when this picture was taken.

10.9.65

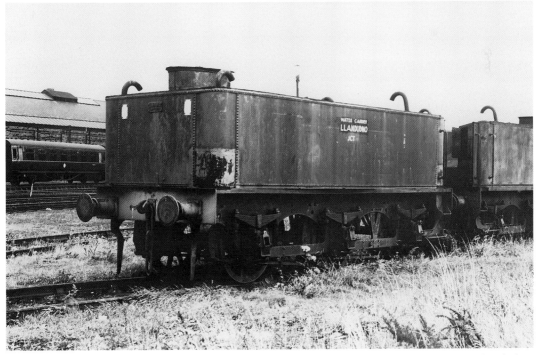

Many old tenders were pressed into service as water carriers. These two were to be seen at Llandudno Junction. Nos 1188 and 1319 were both from withdrawn LNWR 0–8–0s. Both had been stencilled with their function and location.

10.9.65

Transporting the sludge produced by water-softening plants was an ideal job for suitably converted tenders from withdrawn locomotives. This massive eight-wheeled example, pictured at Bletchley, was originally used in company with one of the Lancashire & Yorkshire Railway 0–8–0s introduced by Aspinall in 1903. One of these also ran with the now-preserved ex-LNWR G2 no. 49395 for a time in the mid-1930s.

9.5.65

Much of the side of this 20-ton 'Grampus' ballast wagon was taken up with numbers and signs.

9.5.65

One of the most memorable sights – and sounds – on the railways in the 1950s and 1960s was a loose-coupled goods train. Thousands of wagons such as M 360532, seen here loaded with coal, were in service. Such wagons were an important part of our railway history.

8.9.59

Typical of a huge number of vans in service on British Railways during the 1950s and 1960s, this example, no. M 229051, is a 12-tonner. Long since gone are the mixed goods with their wide variety of vehicles.

1.7.56

In the late 1950s the increasing number of diesel locomotives in service soon resulted in tank wagons appearing at depots. This one, operated by the Mobil Oil Company, was photographed at Bletchley. The small star-shaped plate on the frame registers it as a BR (M) wagon with a 14-ton load capacity.

9.5.65

Opposite, top: Another 14-ton tank wagon photographed at Bletchley was this Mobil example, BRT 5273.

9.5.65

Opposite, bottom: Lettering reading Charringtons can just be seen on the tank side of this 14-ton wagon at Bletchley. Steam was still very much in evidence there when this picture was taken, although the diesel standing next to the wagon was one of several on shed.

9.5.65

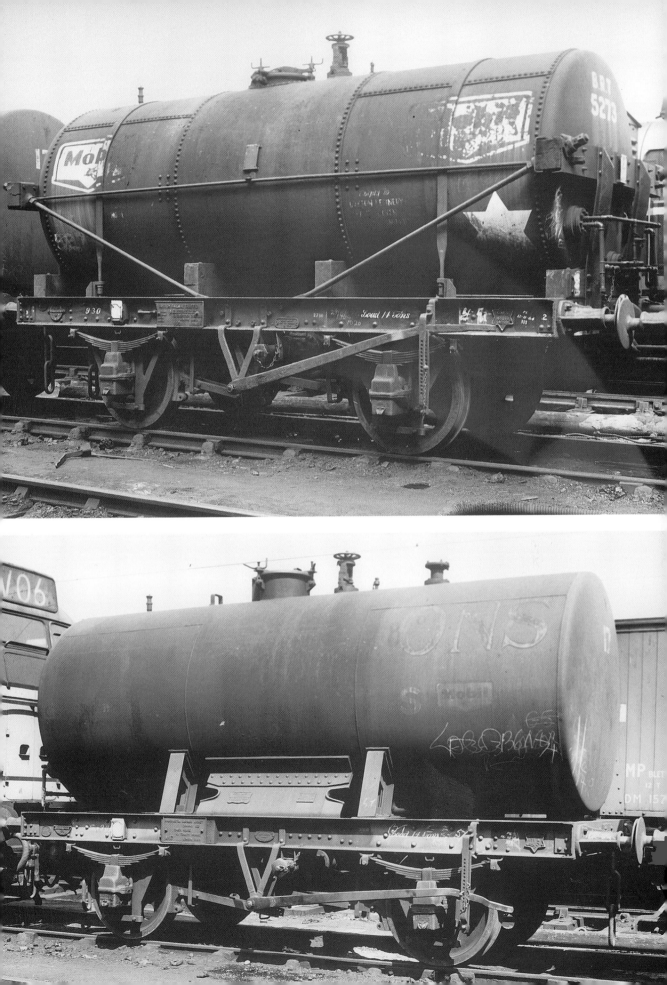

Private scrapyards were involved with cutting up huge numbers of rolling stock as well as the locomotives. No. M 9472M was in quite good external condition as it awaited its fate at Cohens of Kettering. It was built in 1938 at Derby as an open third to diagram 1999. This was the last of its batch.

14.2.65

This cafeteria coach M 256M, pictured at Cohens scrapyard, Kettering, had quite an interesting history. It was built as a 60ft third-class sleeping car, no. 512. During the Second World War many of these coaches were used in ambulance trains, and few, if any, ever ran as sleeping cars again as they were surplus to requirements. No. 512 was converted to a cafeteria coach in 1955 at Eastleigh works. All vehicles of its original design (2195) were withdrawn between December 1964 and November 1965. The side nearest the camera was the cafeteria side, hence the absence of windows over much of its length.

14.2.65

5. The Railway Infrastructure in the Days of Steam

Most enthusiasts in steam days were interested principally in locomotives and few gave more than a passing glimpse to the railway infrastructure. Long since gone are countless things once taken for granted, such as wayside stations, goods sheds, signal-boxes in most parts and of course semaphore signals. While some do still exist, they have faded into history on most lines. Then there were the telegraph poles, something you always had to consider when taking pictures, and of course signs, mostly in cast-iron and many fascinating in themselves. Some referred to the pre-Grouping companies or joint lines, long since forgotten. While my principal interest was locomotives I did recall on film a few of the items that caught my eye – how I wish that I had taken more.

The view up the famous Lickey incline. Over the years a number of locomotive types were used as bankers, and none was more famous than the 0–10–0 no. 58100 known as 'Big Bertha' and built by the Midland Railway especially for this job.
17.7.55

This view looking north from Bedford station shows signals of several types. The main lines and locomotive depot are to the left. Just past the signal-box a 2–6–2T stands in the carriage sidings.

23.6.54

The British Railways locomotive testing station was situated to the south of the Rugby locomotive depot. In front of the building stands a row of empty wagons. Extensive testing of the British Railways Standard steam designs was done at this test plant.

22.7.56

Llandudno station showing no. 2 signal-box together with an array of signals. Two small boys can be seen at the end of the platform eagerly awaiting the next arrival.

12.8.52

Rugby looking north, with its maze of tracks and signals, some of which were colour lights. The tall signal-box can be seen in the distance and on the right is a ventilated six-wheeled coach.

29.5.54

The signalman at Huntingdon no. 2 signal-box exchanges the tablet with the fireman of Ivatt 2–6–0 no. 46400 on its journey to Kettering with the early evening train. Huntingdon no. 2 was responsible for the East Coast main line, and a special walkway with gas lighting was provided for the LMR trains.

6.6.52

The turntable at Kettering depot was typical of many to be found at sheds throughout the London Midland Region. A coal brazier with a pile of ash can be seen on the platform, and a locomotive shovel is propped against the lamp.

14.3.65

This interesting bridge on the Kettering line carried the single track over the River Ouse just before the short climb up to Huntingdon East station. The line closed to all traffic in June 1959 and little now remains to indicate that a bridge once existed here.

29.4.54

The section of line between Huntingdon East and St Ives had strict weight restrictions owing to the presence of the wooden trestle bridges over the River Ouse and its backwaters. This picture shows the bridge between Huntingdon and Godmanchester shortly after it had been reduced to single track. Evidence of rot can be clearly seen on the right-hand timbers. When the time came for complete removal the massive timbers proved very difficult to get out of the river. The former site of this old bridge is now part of the busy A14. LMR territory extended to Godmanchester station, which can just be seen in the distance.

8.3.54

The two Sandy stations looking north. On the right is the London Midland Region station, at one time part of the London Midland & North Western Railway. On the left is the former Great Northern Railway station and the East Coast main line. The island platform served both stations, with the signal-box controlling part of the LMR route to and from Cambridge.

29.4.56

The view looking south from Sandy with the Cambridge LMR lines on the left and the East Coast main line to the right. Note the row of cattle wagons in the main-line goods yard and the number of points that can be seen in this picture.

31.7.54

The London Midland Region station at Sandy which gave easy access to the East Coast main line is on the right of this picture. The signal-box at the end of the platform in the distance was responsible for the Cambridge–Bletchley line only.

31.7.54

Kettering station looking north, with the two fast lines to the left. On the right can be seen the lines leading into the locomotive depot, which was immediately behind the railings. The locomotive in the background was an Eastern Region J15 which worked in from Cambridge, usually spending the best part of the day as shed pilot before returning home with its evening train.

11.4.53

Kettering station looking south. On the left are the slow lines, with the Cambridge line bay at the far end. On the right are the Up and Down main lines. All the platforms still had gas lighting. Several of the glass panels had been removed from the roof of the island platform.

11.4.53

Thrapston in Northamptonshire once boasted two railway stations, one on the Peterborough–Northampton line (seen here) and the other on the Kettering–Huntingdon line. Both have long since gone. When this picture was taken the station was already closed but the water crane still remained intact. The station nameboards had gone but little else had been done except for storing materials under the cover of the platform canopy.

3.10.65

One platform of Huntingdon East station, seen here on the right, was part of the London Midland Region territory. Note the sharp curve or check rail which resulted in a 10mph speed restriction. The line closed in June 1959 and all traces of this station have long since gone.

7.10.54

The Kettering line platform at Huntingdon East station, looking towards Huntingdon no. 1 signal-box with the East Coast main line in the background. The platform was on a severe curve, and a 10mph speed restriction notice can be seen on the left.

28.8.54

The London Midland track, formerly on the right, had completely gone when this picture was taken at Huntingdon East. Most of the buildings had also been reduced to rubble. The small locomotive shed was still in use, albeit as a store for old crossing-gates. The water crane was also still intact and in working order. All traces of this railway scene have long since gone, disappearing under the very busy A14 and various car parks.

7.4.63

One can only guess at just how many times in its long years of exposure to the elements this trespass sign had received a fresh coat of paint. A Lancashire & Yorkshire and London & North Western Railway joint line example, it referred to acts of 1884 and 1883 respectively, and warned people not to trespass on the railway. The penalty for trespassing was forty shillings – a considerable amount of money in those days! The sign was photographed at Huddersfield.

13.5.56

Opposite, top: In the 1950s and 1960s cast-iron notices were still to be found everywhere. These two warning 'Trespassers will be prosecuted' and 'Beware of trains' were alongside a branch-line crossing. Although they required an occasional coat of paint, these notices were certainly long-lasting, with vast numbers of pre-Grouping origin still to be found.

26.9.53

Opposite, bottom: Years of exposure to inclement weather conditions had taken their toll on this Midland Railway trespass notice. Dated June 1899, it refers to a maximum penalty not exceeding ten pounds for every offence of trespassing on the railway or the works thereof.

5.2.53

MIDLAND RAILWAY

TRESPASSERS
WILL BE PROSECUTED
BY ORDER

BEWARE
OF
TRAINS.

"MIDLAND RAILWAY."
7 Vict. Cap. 18 Sec. 238 enacts "That if any
person shall be or travel or pass upon foot
"upon the Midland Railway without the
"license and consent of the Midland Railway
"Company every person so offending shall
"forfeit and pay any sum not exceeding Ten
"Pounds for every such offence."
Notice is therefore hereby given that all
persons found trespassing upon this Railway
or the Works thereof will be prosecuted.
Alexis L. Charles.
June 1859. Secretary.

Cast-iron notices were produced by the railway companies in vast quantities. This Midland Railway sign was located at Bradford Manningham shed. Entrances at many depots were restricted. The supports and sides of the entrance had recently received a liberal coat of whitewash. Illumination was provided by a gas lamp on a rather ornate bracket.

13.5.56